FOURTEEN LETTERS

FOURTEEN LETTERS

ST. ALDHELM OF SHERBORNE

Contents

1 Letter One   1
2 Letter Two   9
3 Letter Three   11
4 Letter Four   17
5 Letter Five   21
6 Letter Six   23
7 Letter Seven   27
8 Letter Eight   29
9 Letter Nine   31
10 Letter Ten   33
11 Letter Eleven   35
12 Eleven Twelve   37
13 Letter Thirteen   39
14 Letter Fourteen   41

Copyright 2024 by Dalcassian Press

All rights reserved. No part of this book may be reproduced in any manner whatsoever without written permission except in the case of brief quotations embodied in critical articles and reviews.

No part of this publication may be reproduced, distributed, or transmitted in any form or by any means, including photocopying, recording, or other electronic or mechanical methods, without the prior written permission of the publisher, except in the case of brief quotations embodied in critical reviews and certain other non-commercial uses permitted by copyright law. For permission requests, write to Dalcassian Press at admin@thescriptoriumproject.com

Translator: Curtin, D.P. (1985-)

ISBN:979-8-3483-0107-1 (Paperback)
ISBN: 979-8-3483-0108-8 (eBook)
Library of Congress Control Number:

Printed by Ingram Content Group, 1 Ingram Blvd, La Vergne, Tennessee
First Printing 2024, Dalcassian Press, Wilmington, DE

This work is part of a series produced in association with the Scriptorium Project and its community of scholars and translators.
Please visit our website at: www.thescriptoriumproject.com

1

Letter One

OF ALDHELM TO GERUNTIUS.

To the most glorious Lord, governing the scepters of the western kingdom, whom I embrace with fraternal charity, as he is a scrutator of hearts and a witness of things, King Geruntius, and to all the priests of God dwelling throughout Domnonia, Aldhelm, serving in the office of abbot without the privilege of merits, wishes health in the Lord.

Recently, when I was in the council of bishops, an innumerable multitude of God's priests gathered from almost all of Britain, especially convened to discuss the decrees of canons and the statutes of the Fathers concerning the care of the Churches and the salvation of souls, and to preserve them in common, with Christ providing protection. Therefore, having duly prayed, the entire priestly council compelled my smallness by the same command and similar sentiment to direct the written letters to your piety, and to intimate their paternal petition and wholesome suggestion through the written style, namely, concerning the unity of the Catholic Church and the concord of the Christian religion, without which it languishes idly, and the future reward withers. For what benefit are the fruits of good works if they are carried out outside the Catholic Church, even if someone diligently practices the actual rule of rigid conduct under the discipline of a monastery, or certainly, avoiding the companionship of all mortals, leads a contemplative life in a remote, squalid solitude? Therefore, so that your sagacity may more certainly perceive for what reasons my mediocrity has directed these writings, I will briefly and concisely explain. Indeed, we have heard and found out through various relative rumors that your priests do not agree in the rule of the Catholic faith, according to the precept of Scripture, and through their disputes and quarrels of words, a serious schism and cruel scandal arises in the Church of Christ, which is testified by the sentiment of the Psalmist, saying: "Great peace have those who love your law, and nothing causes them to stumble." For pious concord joins the peace of religion, just as dire contention contaminates charity. For the Psalmist urges the followers of the right faith to unity of brotherhood, saying: "God makes them dwell together in unity." This house, according to allegory, is understood to be the Church spread throughout the corners of the world. Indeed, heretics and schismatics, being outsiders from the society of the Church, through arguments of contention, flourish in the world, and, like dreadful seeds of tares sown in the midst of a fruitful harvest, they stain the Lord's harvest. But the disgrace of such altercation is restrained by the apostolic trumpet. "If anyone wishes to be contentious," he says, "we have no such custom, nor does the Church of God, which has no stain or wrinkle." Indeed, the evangelical proclamations declare that peace is the mother of Catholics and the mother of the children of God: "Blessed are the peacemakers, for they shall be called sons of God." Hence, when our Lord and Savior descended from the highest height of heaven, to erase the handwriting of the first man and reconcile the world with peace, the angelic melody sang: "Glory to God in the highest, and on earth peace to men of good will." And the Psalmist: "Let there be peace in your strength, and abundance in your towers." Finally, a rumor contrary to the faith of the Church has spread far and wide, that there are certain priests and clerics in your province stubbornly rejecting the tonsure of Saint Peter, the prince of the apostles, and living while stubbornly defending themselves with such an excuse, that they imitate the tonsure of their authors and predecessors, whom they claim to have been illuminated by divine grace with grandiloquent assertions. If they were to inquire from us who was the first author of this shaving and tonsure, they would either fall silent, completely ignorant of the truth, or feign ignorance of falsehood. However, according to the opinion of many, we have learned that Simon, the inventor of magical arts, was the chief of this tonsure, because whatever deceit of necromancy he fraudulently devised against blessed Peter, the contest of the apostles and the ten books of Clement are witnesses. We, I say, according to the sacred authority of Scripture, bearing witness to the truth of our tonsure, assert for various reasons that the apostle Peter took up this rite primarily to bear the form and likeness of Christ on his head, while, for our redemption, he was to undergo the cross, cruelly crowned with sharp thorns by the wicked people of the Jews; then, that the priests of the Old and New Testaments might be distinguished in tonsure and habit; finally, that the same apostle and his successors might bear the ridiculous mockery of barking in the Roman people, because their barons and enemies used to sell those defeated in battle under crowns. Moreover, in the Old Testament, the sign of tonsure was taken from the Nazarenes, that is, the saints, if I am not mistaken. For it is a sign of royal and priestly lineage. For the tiara was placed on the heads of the priests among the ancients. This was round, made of twisted silk, like a central sphere, and this is signified by the part of the head that is shorn. The crown, however, is the breadth of a golden circle that surrounds the heads of kings. Therefore, both signs are expressed on the heads of clerics, Peter saying: "You are a chosen generation, a royal priesthood." This rite of cutting and shaving is marked so that vices may be cut off, and we may be stripped of the hair of our flesh as if of crimes.

However, there is another cruel destruction of souls, which, during the sacred Paschal solemnity, does not follow the rule of 318 Fathers, who established by keen insight the course of the nineteen-year cycle from the Nicene Council, running straight through to the end of the world, by the octad and the undecad. And from the fourteenth moon to the twenty-first, they handed down the series of calculations and the limit of the Paschal calculation, which they deemed unlawful to anticipate or transgress against law and right. Furthermore, these according to the computation of the nineteen-year cycle of Anatolius, or rather according to the rule of Sulpicius Severus, who described the course of eighty-four years, celebrate the Paschal sacrament on the fourteenth moon with the Jews, while neither of the Roman Church's pontiffs follows the perfect calculation of the calendar. Nor did they decree that the course of Victor's Paschal table, which is contained in the cycles of 432 years, should be followed by posterity. For there was a certain kind of heretics among the Easterners, called tessareskaidekatitai, that is, fourteenth-day men, because they celebrate the solemnity of Pascha on the fourteenth moon with the Jews blaspheming Christ and trampling the pearls of the Gospel in the manner of swine, and for this reason, they are considered unfortunate outsiders from the blessed fellowship of the orthodox among the gatherings of schismatics, which I remember blessed Augustine mentioned in his book on ninety heresies. Truly, how greatly this differs from the Catholic faith and discord from the evangelical tradition, that beyond the strait of the river Sabrina, the priests of the Demetians, boasting of their private purity of conduct, greatly abominate our communion, to such an extent that they do not deem it worthy to celebrate the offices of prayer with us in the Church, nor to partake of the dishes of food at the table for the sake of charity: indeed, they throw the fragments of dishes and the remains of meals to be devoured by the jaws and filth of dogs and unclean pigs. They also prescribe that vessels and phials be purified and cleansed with sandy gravel or the yellow ashes of soot. No peaceful greeting is offered, no kiss of pious brotherhood is given, as the Apostle says: Greet one another with a holy kiss, nor is a cloth or water with a towel presented by hands, nor are feet placed in a basin for washing, when the Savior, girded with a towel, washed the feet of His disciples, giving us a model to imitate, saying: Just as I have done, so you also do to others. But indeed, if any of ours, that is, Catholics, go to them for the sake of residing, they are not deemed worthy to be admitted to the fellowship of their society until they are compelled to undergo a period of penance for forty days. And in this, they unfortunately imitate the heretics, who wished to be called Katharos, that is, pure. Alas! alas, for such errors! rather than Evax! Evax! I believe it should be lamented with tearful voices and sorrowful sobs, and all this is known to be done against the precepts of the Gospel according to the empty traditions of the Pharisees, truly attested by Christ (Matthew 23): Woe to you, scribes and Pharisees, who cleanse what is outside the cup and dish. For the Lord is described as having celebrated banquets with publicans and sinners, as a true physician to compose remedies of divine pity and a plaster of heavenly mercy for the festering wounds of souls. Therefore, He did not despise the associations of sinners, in the manner of the Pharisees, but rather mercifully refreshed that sinful woman, lamenting her polluted life, and moistening the Lord's feet with a flood of tears, and wiping them with her loosened and flowing hair, saying (Luke 7:47): Her many sins are forgiven, for she loved much.

Since these matters stand thus, because of the common lot of the heavenly homeland and the assembly of angelic fellowship, relying on prayers and with bent knees, we humbly urge your fraternity, beseeching you, not to disdain further the teachings and decrees of blessed Peter with a stubborn heart and a bold spirit, nor to arrogantly scorn the tradition of the Roman Church, relying on the ancient statutes of your predecessors in a tyrannical obstinacy. For Peter, having confessed the Son of God with a blessed voice, was deemed worthy to hear (Matthew XVI): You are Peter, and upon this rock I will build my Church, and the gates of hell shall not prevail against it, and I will give you the keys of the kingdom of heaven; and whatever you bind on earth shall be bound in heaven, and whatever you loose on earth shall be loosed in heaven. Therefore, if the keys of the heavenly kingdom were bestowed upon Peter by Christ, concerning whom the poet says: The heavenly key-bearer, who opens the gate in the sky; who, despising the principal statutes of his Church and disregarding the mandates of doctrine, joyfully enters through the gate of heavenly paradise? And if he merited to receive the power of binding and the monarchy of loosing in heaven and on earth by a fortunate lot and special privilege, who, rejecting the rule of the paschal feast and the rite of Roman tonsure, would not rather consider himself bound by strict bonds inextricably than to be mercifully absolved? But perhaps any reader of the strophes of books, and a keen debater of scriptures, may defend himself with such a shield of excuse and protect himself with such an apology: I, he says, venerate the precepts of both Testaments with sincere faith, and I confess with a believing heart the one essence of the Holy Trinity, the one substance, and the threefold substance of the persons, I will freely proclaim the sacrament of the Lord's Incarnation, the scaffold of passion, and the trophy of resurrection through the voice of the people. I will diligently announce the supreme judgment of the living and the dead, when each will be weighed with the most equitable scales of judgment according to the diversity of merits, and I will be counted among the congregation of Catholics gathered without any obstacle of misfortune, relying on this privilege of faith. But I will strive to shake and break down the bulwark of this excuse, under which they trust to hide. For James, the son of the Lord's aunt, says: You believe that there is one God, and because he spoke ironically to the twelve tribes established in the dispersion of nations, he immediately added: You do well; even the demons believe, and tremble, for faith without works is dead. Indeed, Catholic faith and the concord of fraternal charity tend inseparably along the same path, as the excellent preacher and chosen vessel elegantly attests (1 Corinthians XIII): If I know all prophecy, and all mysteries, if I have faith so that I could remove mountains, and if I deliver my body to be burned, but do not have charity, it profits me nothing. And to briefly conclude all in a concise statement, he who does not follow the dogma and rule of

Saint Peter boasts in vain about the Catholic faith. For the foundation of the Church and the firmament of faith is primarily placed in Christ and subsequently in Peter, which will not waver or shake under the onslaught of stormy tempests, as the Apostle proclaims (1 Corinthians III, 11): For no one can lay a foundation other than that which is laid, which is Jesus Christ. But the truth has thus sanctioned this privilege of the Church to Peter (Matthew XVI): You are Peter, and upon this rock I will build my Church.

2

Letter Two

ALDHELM TO HIS SISTER OSGITHA.

To my most beloved and dearest sister, and to me venerable with sincere affection of charity, Aldhelm, a humble servant, bearing the unworthy title of abbot, wishes health in the Lord.

Let your highness know that I have asked the bishop about the baptism of my sister, who granted permission to baptize that holy woman, but only secretly and discreetly. I greet you diligently, Osgitha, from the depths of my heart, beseeching with fervent prayers that you do not cease to occupy your mind with the constant meditation of the Scriptures, that you may fulfill the saying of the Psalmist (1:2): In his law he will meditate day and night. And the same Psalmist also testifies saying (119:103): How sweet are your words to my taste! and the rest. As for my prayers, may all the sisters be mindful of them; through Christ I humbly beseech, who says to the apostle (James 5:16): The prayer of a righteous person is powerful and effective. Farewell! ten times dearest, indeed a hundred and a thousand times. May God grant you strength.

3

Letter Three

ALDHELM TO EAUFRID, RETURNING FROM IRELAND TO THE HOMELAND.

To the venerable Eahfrid, greatly honoring the merits of the saints, Aldhelm, a humble servant in the Lord, eternal greetings.

First, let us hymn the panegyric poems proclaiming under the sky, especially for the pious privilege of the foremost of all rulers and magistrates, with a shrill symphony of voices, and with the melody of song, especially because at last the offspring of the blessed mother (due to the inextricable sins of the progenitors) is deemed worthy to obliterate the ancient handwriting of sins, destined for the earth, who cast the lurid, three-pronged hydra, spewing forth rancid and virulent poisons throughout the ages, into the depths of Tartarus. And where previously the raw fawns of that infamous mother were worshipped in foolishness in the temples, now, in turn, the disciples' whirlpools (indeed the sacred abodes of the blessed) are skillfully constructed by the ingenuity of the architect.

I confess, as a client of brotherhood and a citizen of a high municipality, after we learned that your ambrosial return had safely reached the shores of Britain from the stormy climates of the island of Ireland (where it had been nourished for about three times seven years in the rich circle of wisdom), and with the report of the rumor bearers, we immediately offered ineffable thanks to the high heavens (as the burning and blazing love demanded), spreading our wings on high and dancing; especially because you deemed it worthy to bring back the exiled client of the ancient rural patronage (across the blue sea of green, and the enormous stones of the dodrant and the foamy nymphs of the water, sailing the stormy waves with a ship's keel), with the captain rejoicing; so that when you had long ago grown up from the rudiments of infancy to the age of maturity, now in turn (supported abundantly by the favor of the heavens) returning from the habitation of a foreign land, you may function relying on the call of a teacher assigned and chosen.

I do not wish to hide from your blessedness that I have grown greatly in the depths of my heart (for the increase, as I believe, is a dance for the mysteries, indeed for the glory of the name of Kyrios): that a proclamation beyond measure has emerged in the Scottish land where you dwell (in whose company you have relied for a while), as if with a certain thunderous noise emerging from a stormy cloud, our ears are shaken, and throughout the vast expanses of the earth, the opinion of reading, spread among towns and provinces, increases. Indeed, the flow is so frequent (from this side to that, from here to there) across the navigable waters of the surging waves, like a certain community of bees producing nectar. For just as alternately, while the mist of night withdraws, the honeyed swarm (emerging from the heavenly axis to the heights of the Titan) carries away the fragrant burdens through the flowering linden trees, to the slender gates, so too, if I am not mistaken, the gathering of readers (dunning tac fridh) and the remaining keen group of students, from the flowering fields of hagiography, not only take up the arts of grammar and geometry, three times omitted the machines of physical art, but also partake of the more important allegorical and tropological discussions, drawing from the enigma-laden problems of the shadowy mysteries, and in the hives of wisdom, maintaining a constant meditation, they withdraw. From this catalog, your skillful journey, laden with spoils and overflowing with the torrent of the flowing holy, has spread an excellent reputation.

Therefore, I beseech your affable discipleship, as one who is bowed down with knees bent in prayer, to ensure that the forgotten memory does not pass away, that the Pacific, endowed with heavenly ambrosia (substituted by the father by hereditary right, serving as the scepter of the Israelite people for four times four cycles of time), has brought forth by the nourishing breath, saying: Drink water from your cistern, and the streams of your well; let your fountains be dispersed abroad, and divide your waters in the streets; let them be yours alone, and let no stranger partake with you. Therefore, imbued with these sacred inspirations, open the deep well of orthography with constant effort, and water the thirsty fields of minds, so that the seed of heavenly existence (born from the sweat of the sower in the orthodox furrows) may thrive without any scorching obstacle of drought, and abundantly, by God's favor, the harvest may finally mature. For this reason, the humble supplicant is seen to have suggested this prayer so earnestly, that some are known to be endowed with heavenly wisdom, and enormously filled with secret light; however, they have not fully proclaimed (with the treasury of knowledge opened) but have generously given in parts to the readers. For (according to the authority of the Gospel) the burning lamp is not hidden in the dark corner of the urn, which ought to shine with clear light from the top of the candlestick; nor is the talent of the buried talents wasted in the hidden sands, which ought to be cast out for the numerous coins of the money changers; lest, like a sluggish servant (lazy and torpid), he be thrown into the utmost squalor of the prison; but rather let him rejoice and enter into the dance proposed by the pious proclaimer. Hence the Psalmist, to expiate the sin of his own conscience, begins with a sacred prophecy: I have not hidden your righteousness, and the rest.

But as this miserable little man rolls out these words, I was shaken by a double scruple; why, I say, is Ireland, where readers are brought together in groups from here, raised up by some ineffable privilege, as if there could be no teachers of Argive or Roman citizens found there, who could unravel the problems of the heavenly library for the inquiring scholars? For although the aforementioned rural Ireland, flourishing with the wealth of learners, as I might say, nourished by the abundant numbers of readers, just as the poles are adorned with the shimmering vibrations of the stars, yet the climate of Britain, situated at the extreme edge of the western world (for example) enjoys the splendid appearance of the fiery sun and the bright moon; that is, Theodore, serving in the pontifical office, from the very beginning of the rudiments in the flourishing of the philosophical art, and also the same client of that brotherhood, Adrian, endowed with ineffable urbanity.

And boldly contesting in the open, disregarding the frivolous allure of falsehood, I will discern with the fair scale of truth; even if Theodore of blessed memory, governing the helm of the highest priesthood, is surrounded by a multitude of Hibernian disciples (or a fierce boar of the Molossi, fenced in by the ringing of the platform), skillfully wielding the sharpened tooth of grammar (lacking the loss of expense), shakes off the rebellious phalanxes, and (as a warrior in the midst of the field, surrounded by the thick phalanxes of rivals) soon, with the sinewy flight of his arms drawn like a bow, and with spears drawn from the quiver, that is, with the opaque and sharp syllogisms of the Chronography; the swelling troop of arrogance, having lost the tortoise of maidens, turning their backs, hastily seeks the dark hiding places of caves, with the victor triumphing.

Yet let no one presume to vilify the Scottish scholars, whose gemmed sagacity of dogmas your insight has somewhat abused, since I was striving to weave the proclamation of our own amiably, not mockingly rumoring your ridicule, but rather, in the manner of jesters and scurrilous speakers, caviling under the pretense of fraternal irony of love. If, however, anything, supplied by ignorance, is found to have been brought forth by a garrulous page, as the versifier says:

Let it be worthy of the fleeing fumble of the speaker:

Let not the writer fear to seize the terrifying sheets,
As a shaggy goat gnaws the grapes with its teeth;
Nor do they correct the stumbling grammar of the poet.

4

Letter Four

OF ALDHELM TO BISHOP HEDDA.

To the most reverend Lord, and to all the venerable exertions of virtues, and after God, to a special patron, your humble servant in the Lord sends greetings.

I confess, O most blessed prelate, that I had long ago decided, if the course of things and the fleeting change of times permitted, to celebrate the neighboring solemnity of the desired Nativity of the Lord, rejoicing in the company of brethren there, and afterward to enjoy the presence of your charity as a companion in life. But because we have been delayed by various obstacles of impediments, as the bearer of these presents will more fully proclaim by word of mouth, we could not accomplish that; therefore, I beseech you to grant pardon for this difficulty. For not small intervals of time are to be postponed in this study of reading for him alone who, inflamed by the sharpness of reading, will delve into the laws of the Romans to the marrow, and will search all the secrets of the jurists from the innermost recesses, and, what is much closer and more perplexing, to discern the hundred kinds of meters by a pedestrian rule, and to survey the added melodies of song along the straight path of syllables. For readers studious of this matter, the obscurity presented is so much more inextricable, as the rarity of learned men is found. But to discuss these matters in a lengthy span of words is not at all permitted by the narrowness of epistolary communication, how indeed the clandestine instruments of the very art of metrics are conglomerated with letters, syllables, feet, poetic figures, verses, tones, and times; also how the discipline of the sevenfold division of poetry, that is, acephals, lagaros, protilos, along with others, is varied; which verses are monoschemi, which pentoschemi, which decaschemi, are measured by a certain measure of feet; and by what reasoning catalectic, brachycatalectic, or hypercatalectic verses are recognized by keen argumentation. These things, as I believe, and similar matters, cannot be grasped in a brief interval of time and momentary impulse.

But what should be mentioned regarding the method of calculation? when such an imminent despair of computation has oppressed the neck of my mind, that I would regard all the past labor of reading as little, which I had believed I knew in its secret chambers; and to use the sentence of blessed Jerome, who before seemed to me a little wise, I began again to be a disciple, when the opportunity was offered, and thus finally, relying on heavenly grace, I found the most difficult arguments of things and the computations of calculations, which are called parts of numbers, through the insistence of reading. Moreover, regarding the zodiac and the twelve signs, which revolve in the whirl of the heavens, I think it best to remain silent, lest a dark and profound matter, which requires a long explanation, should be brought to light if it is revealed by a trivial series of interpretation, and thus become infamous and cheapened, especially since the expertise of astrological art and the perplexed computation of horoscopes require the elaboration of a more learned investigation.

For this reason, dearest Father, I have briefly touched upon these matters, not drawn in by the clamor of garrulous verbosity, but so that you may know that such arcana of things cannot be understood unless frequent and lengthy meditation has been applied.

Salute in Christ all my band of companions from the least to the greatest, whom I beseech and adjure by the mercy of Christ to pour forth prayers to the Lord for me, oppressed by the weight of sins and the burden of crimes.

5

Letter Five

OF A CERTAIN ANONYMOUS SCOT TO ALDHELM, ABBOT OF MALMESBURY.

To the holy Lord, the most wise, indeed most beloved in Christ, Aldhelm; a Scot of unknown name in God eternal, greetings.

While I do not doubt that I prefer to learn from your mouth, the source of pure knowledge, rather than to drink from any other turbulent master, I know you are distinguished by your talent, Roman eloquence, and the varied bloom of literature (even in the Greek manner). Know this, foreseeing, that for this reason I confidently implore you to receive me and teach me, since the brilliance (as it is said) of wisdom flees before many in you, and you know the minds of foreigners who desire to learn wisdom: because you have been a stranger in Rome, moreover, that you were nurtured by a certain holy man of our kind. These reasons should suffice for brevity, for if you will humbly attend through charity, you will perceive no less through a few words than through many discourses. I sincerely discuss these things with you. You have a certain little book, which is not greater than a two-week allowance, which I wish to cover. I mention this brief time, not because I need more, but lest this request create weariness in your mind. I also hope to obtain a servant and horses, as I think. In this time of harvest, I will hope for a joyful response from you. May your blessedness be deemed worthy to be guarded by divine grace for us,

> O Christ, powerful creator of things,
> Voice of the highest sense of God, whom the Father poured forth from the high
> Mind, and granted such a sharing of the kingdom.
> You subdued the impious crimes of our life,
> Having suffered in bodily form to clothe the world,
> And to speak openly to the peoples, and to confess man.
> Whom, enclosed in the womb of Mary, soon with divinity seen,
> The virgin's bosom trembled, and the unmarried mother
> Was astonished to fulfill her hidden womb with birth,
> To bear her author, mortal hearts
> Weaving the artificer of the sky, and the discoverer of the world,
> Was part of the human race, and lay hidden under one
> Breast, which embraces the whole world widely.
> And who, neither in the spaces of the earth, nor in the waves of the sea,
> Nor captured in heaven, flowed into small limbs,
> But also endured the name of suffering and the bond,
> So that you might snatch us from death, and flee from death
> By your death, soon lifted into the ethereal airs,
> Returning to the joyful light of the parent,
> May you cherish the August one as often on festive days,
> That the annual fasts of the sacred may celebrate sincerely.

6

Letter Six

OF ETHELWALD TO ALDHELM.

To the most holy abbot Aldhelmus, to me bound by the knots of inextricable burning love, as merits demand, Ethelwald, a humble pupil of your pious fatherhood, perpetual health in the Lord.

During the course of the summer season, in which this most wretched homeland is mournfully devastated by the envy of the ravager through immense expeditions of wild beasts, I was lingering with you in the pursuit of reading. Then, may it be for me unworthy, your sacred sagacity, as I believe, has almost entirely revealed the mysteries of the liberal arts studies, obscured only by the thick veil of foolishness, to all, as it were, imbued with the eloquence of both secular literary verbosity and the style of ecclesiastical doctrines written in most fully elaborated volumes. To the complete banquet of overflowing genius, eagerly consumed by the thirsting jaws of understanding, it abundantly refreshed my still pale languor of dullness, promising to nourish me with every instrument of desired reading, which he had recognized as particularly sufficient for my mediocrity, willingly instructing me. Therefore, my most beloved teacher of pure education, as you may easily apply the faith of words with consequent affection, I deem it worth the effort, spurred on by such oracles of sacred Scripture (Prov. VI, 1): "My son, if you have pledged for your friend, you have bound your hand to a stranger, you are ensnared by the words of your mouth." And now I say, if you do not remember yourself entangled in the perplexing restraints of the promised proclamation, yet when you have nurtured me from the very tender cradle of infancy, cherishing, loving, and gradually refreshing me with more delicate foods of skill until you have brought me to vigorous puberty, it is judged worthy by all of sound understanding, that, having already been nourished by the food of a more tender genius, you should also provide me with more solid sustenance of deeper wisdom. However, if the most humble insistence of devoted subjection urgently seeks to provide abundant feasts, you should not deny to bestow; and although you consider me of no importance, do not refuse to enrich your adopted offspring from the abundant wealth of all paternal wisdom for a time; lest at any time the audacious rivals, in a mocking laugh of desired disapproval, rejoice in their triumph, if they find a descendant of opulent paternal philosophy experiencing the impoverishment of foolishness. And it is not incongruous for me to be compared to that Rehoboam, born of the noble lineage of the most famous and praiseworthy wisdom, as well as the rich resources of King Solomon, who, born of an unfortunate origin, is almost entirely devoid of all paternal happiness, and can be mournfully equated. Finally, now about to fulfill my vows, and hastily complete the benefit of the abundant education, knowing that you will undoubtedly gain a greater glory of perpetual reward from it, with the Lord assisting, because (Matt. X) "he who endures to the end will be saved." To this letter of our smallness, I have submitted three songs of a sung melody, arranged in two kinds, of which the first is elaborated in the dactylic hexameter of heroic poetry and pedestrian, as I say, and measured and in the forms of 70 verses, occurring by chance, and, to speak more truly, divided by the nod of heavenly dispensation. The third also is not elaborated in foot measure, but composed of eight syllables in each verse, adapted with the same letter to the paths of the lines, hastily written for you, most sagacious sower. I have presented the middle one, composed of the most similar lines of verses and syllables, to my and your client Winfrid regarding the pilgrimage of the overseas journey. I deemed it necessary for your blessedness to be represented with venerable eyes, as it seemed worthy in the judgment of our smallness, to first reveal the little work of my letters to you, as a Father, so that, having been proven by the probable judgment of your sublimity and derived to the standard of equity, it may be acceptable to all subsequent numbers of readers. Farewell in Christ.

7

Letter Seven

ALDHELM TO ADRIAN.

To the most reverend Father and my venerable teacher of my rudimentary infancy, Adrian, Aldhelm, a native of the family of Christ and a humble pupil of your piety, greetings, etc.

I confess, my dearest, whom I embrace with the grace of pure affection, after having departed from your social company about three years ago, I have been separated from Kent, that our smallness has long been burning with ardent desire for your company; which I have also long considered, as is in my vows, to fulfill if the course of affairs and the vicissitudes of times would allow, and unless various obstacles of impediments would delay me, especially since I was not allowed by the frailty of bodily health, with my members inwardly wasting away, to return home, which once, when I was again with you after the first elements, I was compelled to do.

8

Letter Eight

CELLANUS TO ALDHELM.

To the lord Aldhelm, archimandrite of the Saxons, enriched with studies and adorned with honeyed writings, Cellanus, born in the island of Ireland, hiding in the farthest corner of the limits of the Franks, an exile, a lowly slave of the famous colony of Christ, in the whole and safe Trinity, greetings.

Almost like a penny, the rumor of your Latin panegyric has reached the ears of our poverty, which the agile readers do not dread hearing without a jest or the imposture of amurca, known for the beauty of the Alburnus of Romania. And if we have not earned the merit of hearing you in person, we have nonetheless read your good deeds, constructed like a lance, depicted in the fasti of various delights of flowers. But if you restore your heart with sad foreign things, send forth a few little words from those most beautiful lips of yours, from whose purest fountain many may refresh their minds, to the place where Lord Furseus rests in holy and entire body.

9

Letter Nine

A FRAGMENT OF ALDHELM'S LETTER TO CELLANUS.

I marvel that such a small man from the famous and flourishing countryside of the Franks interrupts your industrious fraternity of Saxons, born of noble lineage and cradled under the Arctic pole in the tender swaddling clothes of infancy.

10

Letter Ten

ALDHELM TO ETHELWALD.

To my most beloved son and fellow disciple Ethelwald, Aldhelm, the least of the servants of God, greetings.

Just as I have cared to admonish you in person a few times about certain matters, so now, relying on paternal authority according to God, I am not reluctant to exhort you in writing while you are absent. For we do this because the love of Christ, as the Apostle says, compels us. Therefore, my dearest son, although you exist in the youth of age, do not let yourself be overly subjected to the vain pleasures of this world, whether in the more frequent and prolonged use of daily drinks and feasts in an unbecoming excess, or in the culpable wandering of horsemanship, or in any pleasures of bodily delight that should be abhorred. Always remember what is written: Youth and pleasure are vain. I also admonish you not to serve excessively the vehement money and all the detestable vanity of worldly glory, remembering that saying: What does it profit a man if he gains the whole world, but suffers the loss of his soul? For the Son of Man will come in his glory and that of the holy angels; and he will repay each according to his works. But much more, my most beloved, always be vigilant in divine readings and sacred prayers. If you truly strive to know anything further from secular letters, do it only for this reason, that since in divine law the text of words consists almost entirely of grammatical reasoning, you may understand the most profound and sacred meanings of that divine eloquence more easily by reading, the more fully you have learned the various rules of that reasoning by which it is woven [...] Do not fail to always keep this letter among the other books you read, so that by its most frequent reading of what is written in it, you may be reminded in my stead. Farewell.

11

Letter Eleven

ALDHELM TO THE CLERGY OF BISHOP WILFRID.

Recently, the furious disturbance of a storm, as you have learned by experience, shook the foundations of the Church, as if by a tremendous earthquake; whose noise resounded through various regions of the earth, like the thunderous crash, far and wide. And therefore I implore you, my heartfelt brethren, with your knees bent, not to be scandalized by this disturbance, lest anyone of you become sluggish in faith through mental lethargy, even if necessity requires that with your own bishop you be driven from the height of pontifical office to the private earth of a father, and everyone must attack the foreign rural realms. For who, I ask, is so hard or cruel in labor that separates you from that bishop; who has nurtured you from the very rudiments of learning and from the tender infancy of early age to the bloom of adult maturity, teaching, correcting, and advancing you in piety; and just as a nurse, with outstretched arms, has lovingly embraced you in the bosom of charity. Please consider the order of creatures and the divinely implanted nature in them; so that from the collection of the smallest things, you may, with Christ's help, capture a flexible form of compassion; how swarms of bees, warmed by the heavenly heat, eagerly emerge from their hives filled with nectar, and, when their leader leaves, the winter homes of the dense caverns, in rapid flight to the ether, except for the guardians of ancient seats for the propagation of future offspring; I say, left behind, more marvelous to tell, the king of them, surrounded by thick ranks of comrades, departs from the winter camp in herds and searches the hollow trunks of trees, if he has been hindered by the dusty spray of sand or delayed by sudden rains dripping from Olympus, and returns to the pleasing basket and original seat, the entire army immediately breaks through the accustomed entrances, joyfully entering the ancient cloisters. [...] If therefore such a creature, devoid of reason, which life and nature govern without written laws, obeys the command of a leader through the reciprocal succession of times, I ask you, does it not seem a horrendous abomination to reproach those who, endowed with the granted sevenfold grace of the Spirit, break the reins of devoted subjection in a frenzied manner? But why, gathering the reasonings of various matters, shall I traverse with a shrill pen to incite the depths of your hearts, listen. Behold, secular exiles from divine knowledge, if they have deserted the devoted Lord whom they loved in prosperity, with the abundance of happiness ceasing, and the adversity of calamity pressing, and have preferred the secure sweet leisure of a rejoicing homeland to the pressure of their Lord, are they not led by all into execrable laughter and the noise of barking? What then will be said of you, if you abandon the bishop who has nourished you and raised you in exile alone? Etc.

12

Eleven Twelve

ALDHELM TO WINBERT.

To the Lord, most beloved of the Lords, Winbert, Aldhelmus, servant of the servants of God, greeting from the stone at the corner of the two testaments, cut from the summits of the mountains, which has crushed a statue made of four types of metal, marking the legs of the four kingdoms of peoples, with a golden head.

We have sent a letter of cerulean ink to your piety, which will fully proclaim to you by word of mouth the cause of our impending necessity, namely concerning the land that the venerable patrician Baldredus offered to us for possession at an agreed price, especially for the capture of fish in a suitable and competent place. And therefore, while it seems to be given and granted in the power of our king, we earnestly pray that we may firmly obtain and hold that same part of the land through the patronage of your charity, lest we be deprived of that possession by violence from the private, since often the rights of justice are shaken and we are defrauded, etc.

13

Letter Thirteen

ALDHELM TO WILFRID.

To the Lord, venerably beloved and delightfully revered, Wilfrid, Aldhelmus, a humble native in Christ, eternal greetings.

It has been reported to me by the rumor-bearers about the industriousness of your charity that you have decided to undertake a journey overseas, guided by the Lord, ignited by the sharpness of reading. And therefore, with life as your companion, holding the desired port of Ireland, especially rejecting the false predictions of philosophers, I read. For I consider it absurd to take a journey through the slippery, overgrown paths of the rough countryside, indeed through the difficult twists of the philosophers, having spurned the inextricable norm of the old and raw Instrument. Or, certainly, you would have to drink from the clear waters of glassy springs, wading through muddy marshes; in which a dark swarm of toads swarms together, and the chatter of croaking frogs resounds. What, I ask, does the sacrament of orthodox faith bring concerning the rash incest of filthy Proserpina, which I abhor to speak of, reading and scrutinizing it closely, or the lewd Hermione, daughter of Menelaus and Helen, who, as ancient works tell, was betrothed long ago by the right of dowry to Orestes, and finally, with a changed sentence, married Neoptolemus, venerating her through the proclamation of reading; or the priests of the Luperci, reveling in the rites of Priapus, to inscribe in heroic style the history; which, once presented at the height of the scepter in the eyes of Hebrew caution, that is, the soul fixed to the wood of the gibbet, utterly vanished down to the ground? Moreover, I request your discipleship, as a humble man with bent knees and flexible limbs, pressed by a foul reputation, to not frequent the brothels of the harlots, in which the pompous harlots hide, indulging in luxurious pleasures, but rather to enjoy your fraternity happily in a humble retreat, disregarding the lofty heights of the hall, which the patricians and praetors possess; nor to neglect against the cold blasts of winter winds emerging from the northern climate, as Christ's discipline teaches, to use a thin garment of cloth rather than a coarse covering.

14

Letter Fourteen

OF BLESSED ALDHELMS, TO ALL CONGREGATIONS PLACED UNDER HIS GOVERNANCE.

On the Freedom of One's Own Election.

Nothing in this world enjoys prolonged happiness, nothing holds a long dominion, nothing seems to tend towards the fatal end of life at a swift pace. And therefore, so we may enjoy the inheritances of worldly things, that we may never be defrauded of the benefits of the eternal homeland. Hence it is that I, Aldhelmus, after I, unworthy and unproven by any worthy morals, had been placed in the seat of the pontifical office by divine grace, proposed with a secret affection of my mind that in my monasteries, Maildunesburg, Frome, Bradanford, where I have long since been established in the rank of abbot, with the Lord's support, I would have a religious abbot, whom the spontaneous choice of my families would elect with a harmonious voice, to be established by canonical creation and regular sanction. My voluntary propositions were met with the stubbornness of my monks; and although I have often narrated this diligently in the assembly of my brothers, no one gave the most peaceful assent to my wishes, saying: As long as you are alive and vigorous in spirit, you are dedicated to the study of this present life, we do not disdain to humbly submit our necks under the yoke of your dominion. But this we humbly and communally beseech, that under the sacred testimony of the Scriptures and the clear consent of favorable men, you strengthen that no one after your death, neither royal audacity nor pontifical authority, nor any man of ecclesiastical or secular dignity, may claim leadership over us without our will.

I willingly consented to the petition of my monks, especially the servants of God; and in the monastery that is near the river called Wenburnia, which is presided over by the venerable sister of our king, Cuthberga, with the desirable consent of the most famous king Inii, and the devoted approval of my reverend brother and co-bishop Daniel, I confirmed the most decent petition of the Lord's servants with the sign of the sacred cross. Likewise, the same venerable king and the aforementioned bishop subscribed with equal devotion. Not long after, in the sacred council, which is known to have been convened near the river called Wodor, the authority of all the archimandrites of the Saxon people, with the assent of royal power and the nod of the pontifical prior, agreed. If anyone, however, should plot against the decrees of such illustrious persons and presume to violate the sacred provisions of this present document, let him know that he will be struck down before the terrible throne of divine Majesty, along with the transgressors of the Lord's commandments, by a mournful judgment of condemnation. This charter of confirmation was written from the Incarnation of our Lord Jesus Christ, in the third indiction.

+ *Sign of the hand of Bishop Daniel.*
+ *Sign of King Inii.*
+ *Sign of the hand of the patrician Ethelred.*

This work was produced in association with:

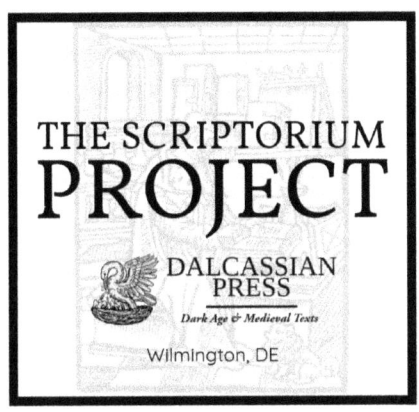